AUSS!E
ENGLISH

AUSSiE ENGLISH

an explanation of the Australian idiom

by JOHN O'GRADY
(Nino Culotta)

Illustrated by WEP

LANSDOWNE PRESS
Sydney · Auckland · London · New York

Published by Lansdowne Press, Sydney.
a division of RPLA Pty Ltd
176 South Creek Road, Dee Why West, NSW, Australia 2099
First published 1965
25th Impression 1983
© Copyright John O'Grady 1965, 1973
Produced in Australia by the Publisher
Printed in Hong Kong by Everbest Printing Co., Ltd.

National Library of Australia Cataloguing-in-Publication Data
O'Grady, John, 1907-1981
    Aussie English.

    First published: Sydney: Ure Smith, 1972.
    ISBN 0 7018 1585 x.

    I. Title.

A823'.3

Preface

AUSTRALIANS speak English. They don't speak it like Englishmen, or Scotsmen, or Welshmen, or Irishmen, or Americans, or Canadians, or South Africans, or Indians, or Pakistanis—or anybody else you can think of who speaks, or claims to speak, English. They speak their own brand of the language, developed during their years of isolation from other English-speaking peoples. Whom they can understand.

But most other English-speaking people have difficulty in understanding Australians. And this, to an Australian, is an astonishing thing. After all, his language is uniform. He has no dialects. With a few minor variations in idiom and tempo, his language is the same from Cooktown to Perth, whether you travel around the top, or through the centre, or via the southern cities.

So why do visitors have difficulty in interpreting Aussie statements and questions?

There are three kinds of Australians to be considered:
(1) ORIGINAL AUSTRALIANS. Known as Aborigines, or Abos. The original spear-throwing owners of the

v

country by right of occupation. But largely dispossessed by lead-throwing and disease-distributing characters from the British Isles, who were the ancestors of

(2) OLD AUSTRALIANS. The native-born, locally educated majority of the country's citizens, currently being infiltrated by

(3) NEW AUSTRALIANS. Born in other countries, and speaking their own brand of English or other language, to the annoyance and embarrassment of their Australian-born children.

You won't meet many Original Australians, unless you have the time, patience, endurance and funds to go 'outback'. And even then, very few of them will talk to you. But if they do, they will use English simple enough to give you no trouble.

You will meet some New Australians — whatever part of the world you come from, others from that part are already here — but they will not be of much help to you in interpreting Aussie English, the language spoken by the great majority, Group 2, Old Australians.

This little book is designed to give you some advance information, which should help you to understand what is said to you.

Don't worry about Aussies not understanding you. Whatever kind of English you use, they'll understand it all right. But nothing on this earth will make them imitate it. So you will have to learn to live with their alien sounds. And alien you will discover them to be.

Aussie English has very little music in it. It is generally delivered in tones as tuneless as the bleat of a sheep, or the kark of a questing crow. It is delivered through an almost closed mouth, with a slurring of consonants. And it is delivered as rapidly as possible. Except 'outback', where it is often delivered as slowly as possible.

Its vowel sounds have been compared to those of the London Cockney. But Cockneys feel themselves insulted by the comparison. And so do Australians.

At its worst, it is a mumbled monotone, its sentences slangy, idiomatic, and brief.

At its best, it is clearer, lengthier, grammatically correct — but the unmistakable flat accent will distinguish it from any other intonation on earth.

Your problems are going to be (1) to tune your ear to the accent, so that you may distinguish the words used; (2) to understand the meaning of what you have heard; and (3) to avoid giving offence, or being offended, by expressions whose meanings differ from your own.

This list of some of the most commonly used words and expressions, with explanations and examples where necessary, does not even pretend to be comprehensive. It is, however, vulgar — in the sense that 'vulgar' means 'of or pertaining to the common people, or general public'. (And often in the other sense, too.)

Aussies are extremely inventive where language is concerned, and part of the fun of talking with them will be — for you — listening for and learning new combinations; new ways of saying things. Ways pungent, succinct, apt, sometimes explosive, frequently profane, and always irreverent.

Australians respect a man for what he is, not for what he represents. Most of them have no respect for constituted authority, very little for tradition, and none at all for the English language.

ACID

This word has the usual international chemical meaning. But to 'put the acid on' a female does not mean that you dab a little sulphuric or hydrochloric behind her ears. It implies a question, and whichever way you phrase it, the answer will most likely be an astonished look, followed by a well-swung arm or handbag.

The answer 'yes' should not be expected.

ACRE

Four thousand eight hundred and forty square yards of earth; or any number of square inches, feet, or yards of backside.

Therefore, 'a kick in the acre' does not mean a kick in four thousand eight hundred and forty square yards of earth.

Female 'acres' are generally referred to as 'rears'.

Girls of good family upbringing — i.e., nicely reared girls — are fairly plentiful. But the occasional one who is

9

'six axe handles across the acre' should either give up wearing shorts and slacks, or go on a diet.

ACT
Common phrases are 'He's bungin' on an act', 'I was only bungin' on an act', etc. To pretend to be something which you are not, is to 'bung on an act'. It is wiser — and safer — to be natural, and speak the truth about yourself.

ANCHOR
The brakes on a motor vehicle. When it's necessary to stop your vehicle suddenly, you 'hit the anchors', or 'throw out the anchor'.

'This galah comes hurtlin' out of a side street — doesn't even look to his right — an' I tell you if I hadn't hit the anchors I'd've been gone a million.'

APPLES
'She's apples.' 'She'll be sweet.' 'She'll be right.' 'She's jake.' Meaning quit worrying, all's well.

ARSE
(Americans spell this word *ass*, because they pronounce it that way. But Aussies use the broad 'a'.) Men use this word to describe the human posterior, particularly when suggesting that certain things should be done to it, or with it.

The word 'backside' is more polite; 'posterior' is very polite; and 'sit-upon' is used only by the extremely genteel.

'Bum' and 'fanny' are very seldom used by anybody.

A lucky or fortunate character is known as a 'tin arse'.

And a statement that such and such a thing happened, may be denied with 'Pig's arse it did.'

ARTIST
There are various kinds of artists — pictorial, literary, musical, etc. — but the most common kind are 'bull artists'. These are great exaggerators of stories, tellers of tall tales and of wild improbable things. They are held in rather high esteem, because they provide something for ordinary citizens to talk about, or to laugh about.

ARVO
Afternoon.

'See ya this arvo.' —

'Wotta ya doin' this arvo?' —

'Reckoned he was gunna deliver 'em last week, an' he doesn't turn up till yesterdy-bloody-arvo.'

A*A*A*A*A*A*A

11

BACK

'That part of a man's body that every other bastard ought to keep orf of.'

If you are requested to 'get off me back, will ya?', then get off it — stop worrying the man.

People who get on your back are people who 'lean' on you; who try to persuade you to do things you don't want to do; who nag at you; who harp on the subject of your deficiencies.

Wives frequently get on a man's back.

'See that hump on me back? That's me missus. She's been on it for years.'

BAG

Any unprepossessing female. But, since beauty is in the eye of the beholder, she who is a bag to one, may be a vision of delight to another.

It is not a good idea to refer to a woman as being 'an old bag' without first learning the other fellow's opinion of her. She may be his wife.

BAG OF FRUIT

A suit. An abomination which, with a tie, is still worn in Australia, even in summer. But the further north you go, the fewer will you see. And right up 'the top end', it would be difficult to find a man who owns one.

BARBECUE

Steak, chops and sausages cooked in the open air 'when the weather's right'. What Americans call a 'cook out'.

Sunday is the favoured day for barbecues, and provided there is enough beer it doesn't matter whether the meat is eaten semi-raw, or charred black. There is always enough beer.

Some people drink tea when they have a barbecue. But this practice is considered eccentric.

BASTARD

An extremely useful noun, as valuable to Australians as the coconut is to Polynesians. You will be told that it is a 'term of endearment'. Friends — male — greet each other with phrases like 'Hullo, y'old bastard, what're ya drinkin'?', or 'Where ya been, y'old bastard?' The privilege, however, is reserved for friends. Any stranger who refers to an Australian as a bastard will need reinforcements.

You may, if you feel like it, refer to yourself as being a 'bit of a bastard', and the definition will be accepted.

If you hear a third person, in his absence, described as being a bastard, the word will not be a term of endearment.

There is a vast difference between friendly bastards and

unfriendly bastards, and there are many other kinds of bastards in between. The best kind is your friend.

Then there's the fellow who's 'not a bad poor bastard'; and the one who is a 'harmless poor bastard'; and the one who is a 'poor stupid bastard' — all of whom are 'not bad bastards when you get to know 'em'. But the fellow referred to as 'that bastard' is indeed a proper bastard, to be avoided if possible.

And the worst kind of all is the 'useless bludgin' bastard', who is fortunately rare 'Useless bludgin' bastards' have no friends at all.

Until — and if ever — you become familiar with all the shades of meaning given to the word 'bastard', it will be better for you to leave it out of your conversation. Otherwise you may acquire a reputation for being a 'know-all bastard', which will mean that you know nothing at all.

Discuss the word, if you like, with anybody. But don't use it — about anybody.

BATTLER

Some men, all their lives, 'get it easy'. They seem to escape the worries, troubles, illnesses and adversities that affect most of us. Others get more than their share of these things, and are 'always in bloody strife'. He who gets it *too* easy could end up like King Farouk. He who gets it too hard could have his spirit broken and become a 'dead beat', a 'drifter', or even a 'bot'.

A man is judged by the way he 'measures up' to life. And the bloke who 'does his best' at all times, the bloke who is an 'unlucky poor bastard' but who can still smile, who can still find reserves of strength and courage to try again — and again — and again — is a 'battler'.

A bloke's wife deserts him: he learns to care for the kid. The kid gets sick and dies; he learns to live alone. His jobs, one after another, 'fold up': he gets other jobs. He's always a 'trier'. And he's walking home one evening, stone cold sober, and he gets knocked down by some drunken idiot behind a wheel, and is taken to hospital with his legs broken. 'The boys' have a 'tarpaulin muster' — they take up a collection for him. Because he's a 'battler', and 'real battlers' always have friends.

Then there's the bloke who's known to be 'just a battler'. He has plenty of friends too, because he's honest, genuine, a hard worker, and it's not his fault that he never seems to get anywhere. But he's always 'good for a quid' if you're in trouble yourself.

'Old Ted'd have plenty tucked away, wouldn't he?'

'Not old Ted, mate; he's just a battler, same as the rest of us.'

BEAUT
Very good. First class. Excellent. The word 'beauty', standing alone and spoken emphatically, is an exclamation of approval.

BEER
That warm sweet weak stuff you get in your country, you won't get in this one. We believe that any brew which is not served ice cold, with a reasonable 'head' on it, and containing a large proportion of alcohol, should not be called beer.

You will like our beer. But until you find your capacity for it — take it easy.

'She puts a gut on ya, an' she can knock ya — but she's a beaut drop.'

In fact, you may ask for a 'beaut drop' if you like. Any barmaid will know what you mean. But she won't know how much of it you want. And until you become familiar with the names of the various containers for this national beverage — names which vary from State to State — your best bet would be to look around the bar, see what others are drinking, and point to a container 'about your size'.

Containers run from five-ounce glasses to eighteen-gallon kegs. There are middies, schooners, ponies, lady's waists, butchers, handles, mugs, jugs, tankards, fives, sevens, pints, bottles, cans large and small, glass cans, stubbies — many names, which have significance in particular localities. If you stay long in one place, you'll soon 'wise up'.

In Sydney, and other parts of New South Wales, you'll learn that there are two kinds of beer — new and old. Your palate will tell you which one you prefer. It may tell you that some of each, mixed in the one glass, would be 'just the shot'. In which case, ask for a 'middy of fifty'.

All palates are different, but 'all beer's good only some's better than others'.

BERLEY

You've 'gone fishin''. You have lines, hooks, sinkers, bait, a knife, good friends, and plenty of beer. Beer is essential. There is a saying — 'The trouble with goin' fishin' is there's always some silly bastard wants to fish.' Well, if this 'silly bastard' wants to catch fish, he'd better have some berley with him. 'Berley' is stuff you scatter on the water, or hang over the side in a bag, to attract fish.

16

You can ask any angler what he uses for berley. He may tell you, if he likes you. But ask a group of anglers, and you'll only start an argument. Everyone has his own idea of what is good berley — for women, as well as for fish.

BILLY
No connection with the 'billy' wielded by a London bobby. You make tea in this one.

It is a tragedy when your old billy wears out, and you have to buy a new one. New billies do not make good tea. A proper billy, loved and cherished and worth its weight in gold, should be battered, blackened by the fires of countless camps, stained by thousands of gallons of strong tea, and should never have been washed.

To make a brew in a billy, you get the water boiling, throw a handful of tea in, and then swing the billy by its handle around and around in vertical circles. This 'settles the tea'.

BITE
A request such as 'Excuse me, sir, but I appear to be temporarily short of cigarettes; would it be presumptuous of me to suggest that I may have one of yours?' would cause an Australian to assume a defensive — or offensive — attitude. He would think you were 'kidding' him. He would think that you were 'slinging off' at his way of speech. He would look at you unblinkingly for a long moment, and then turn to one of his friends and say something like, 'What's wrong with this galah?'

But if you said, 'C'n I bite you for a smoke, mate?', he would hand you his packet and say, 'Sure—help yourself.' Unless he considered you to be a 'bot'. In which case he would probably say, 'Get whatsanamed — buy your own.'

To bite somebody — or to 'put the bite on' somebody — is to request a tangible favour.

A bricklayer, referring to his new labourer, said to the author, 'Soon as he arrived on the job, the bastard bit me for a sub.'

To 'bite the boss for a sub' is to request an advance against wages. On the other hand, if you 'have a shot' at a man, and he 'comes in', or 'bites', you are entitled to feel pleased.

Aussies respect a man who can 'take it'; who can listen to his qualities or actions being derided, without losing his temper. He who cannot — he who is thin-skinned — he who bites — will be verbally persecuted, and will eventually have few friends.

BLACK STUMP

Somewhere over the horizon, north, south, east or west of wherever you happen to be, is the charcoal-covered butt of a long-dead, burnt-out tree. What kind of tree it was originally, is not specified. How long it has been there, is not known.

It marks a boundary. Not a physical boundary, because no one has ever seen it. But it stands as a symbol of the limit of measurable distance. And 'the biggest bastard this side of the black stump' would be a man whose bastardry is as immense as that distance.

The biggest, the best, the smallest, the worst, the silliest, the most stupid, the ugliest, or the most beautiful of anything or anybody 'this side of the black stump' rules out all comparison. Because on the other side of the black stump there is nothing but an infinity of sand-hills, or gibber plains, silent under the life-killing sun, where no man lives, and where no trees grow.

BLIND FREDDY

Blind Freddy is dead, but his spirit lives on, and is frequently called upon to measure the lack of physical or mental perception exhibited by your workmate or companion.

'You still lookin' for that bloody shovel? If it was a dog it'd bite you — even Blind Freddy could see it.' —

'I tell you, mate, the race was rigged — even Blind Freddy could see that.' —

'Haven't you got that job finished yet? Blind Freddy could do it in half the time.'

BLOCK

'What'd old Bill get the sack for?'

'Did his block an' donged the boss.'

'Yeah? What'd he dong the boss for?'

'Buggered if I know. But you know old Bill — always doin' his block about somethin' or other.'

'Blocks' are heads. It's not a good idea to 'do' them. A man should learn to keep his temper. But some men never learn. 'Blockheads', for example. They have heads full of 'standard mix' concrete, and can never learn anything — not even enough to be able to earn enough to be able to buy a 'block' of land.

In New Zealand, a block of land is known as a 'section', but there are just as many blockheads amongst Kiwis as there are amongst Aussies. Don't tell them this, though, or one of them may be tempted to 'knock your block off'. And you'd look silly walking down Pitt Street without a head.

BLOKE

A chap. A fellow. A guy. Anybody. We're all blokes. There are good blokes and bad blokes, but most blokes are all right. Some blokes, of course, are 'not worth feedin' ', but most of the blokes you will meet will be prepared to put their hands in their pockets and buy you a drink — proving that there are more good blokes than bad blokes.

BLOODY

Known as the 'Great Australian Adjective'. You will hear it used frequently, and in peculiar ways, best illustrated by this verse of the author's, which is reprinted here by permission of the Sydney *Bulletin*.

INTEGRATED ADJECTIVE

I was down on Riverina, knockin' round the towns a bit,
An' occasionally restin', with a schooner in me mitt;
An' on one o' these occasions, when the bar was pretty
full
An' the local blokes were arguin' assorted kinds o' bull,
I heard a conversation, most peculiar in its way,
Because only in Australia would you hear a joker say,
'Where yer bloody been, yer drongo? 'Aven't seen yer fer
a week;
An' yer mate was lookin' for yer when 'e come in from
the Creek;

'E was lookin' up at Ryan's, an' around at bloody Joe's,
An' even at the Royal where 'e bloody never goes.'
An' the other bloke said, 'Seen 'im. Owed 'im 'alf a bloody
  quid.
Forgot ter give ut back to 'im; but now I bloody did.
Coulda used the thing me-bloody-self; been orf the bloody
  booze,
Up at Tumba-bloody-rumba shootin' kanga-bloody-roos.'

Now their voices were a little loud, an' everybody heard
The peculiar integration of this adjectival word.
But no one there was laughin', an' me I wasn't game,
So I stood around an' let 'em think I spoke the bloody
  same.
An' one of 'em was interested to ask 'im what he'd got —
How many kanga-bloody-roos he bloody went and shot —
An' the shootin' bloke said, 'Things are crook; the
  drought's too bloody tough;
I got forty-bloody-seven, an' that's good e-bloody-nough.'
An' this polite rejoinder seemed to satisfy the mob,
An' everyone stopped listenin' an' got on with the job,
Which was drinkin' beer and arguin' an' talkin' of the heat,
An' boggin' in the bitumen in the middle of the street;
But as for me, I'm here to say the interestin' news
Was 'Tumba-bloody-rumba shootin' kanga-bloody-roos'.

BLOW-IN
An unwanted stranger — in a small group, or in a community. A 'buttinsky'.
    'Blow-ins' — or more generally 'bloody blow-ins' — are never invited, and seldom forgiven.

'Who was that?'

'Buggered if I know — some bloody blow-in.'

The author once heard an Aboriginal on Cape York refer to white men as 'bloody blow-ins who haven't been here two hundred years yet'.

BLUDGE

A bloke who ceases work — temporarily — could be 'havin' a bit of a bludge'.

A bloke who is temporarily out of tobacco or cigarettes is permitted to 'bludge a smoke'.

But a bloke who does as little work as possible — who 'poles on his mates' — and who is eternally bludging smokes, is a 'bludger'. This is a terrible thing to be.

Both words can give offence, and buy fights, so it's better not to use them. Leave them to the locals, who know when it's safe, and when it isn't.

BLUE

A fight. An unfriendly argument. You can 'bung on a blue' — or 'stack on a turn' — and finish up in hospital, or in jail — the 'clink'.

All blues should be avoided, unless you are naturally pugnacious, with a perverted liking for hospitals and jails.

And 'blue stories' should not be told to women, wowsers, or members of the clergy.

BOMB

The equivalent of American 'heap' or 'jalopy'. Any old motor vehicle; but particularly one of the kind bought, patched up, souped up, and driven by young blokes.

'The biggest nuisances on the roads,' says a neighbour, 'is young blokes in old bombs.'

By extension, any mechanical contrivance that constantly gives trouble to its owner can be called a bomb.

And because of their habits — zeroing in on your vehicle unexpectedly and when least wanted — Sydney's parking police are known as 'bombers', or 'brown bombers'. They are unpopular with all motorists.

BOOZER
The local pub. Also one who visits it too often. Alternatives are 'grog shop', and 'grog artist', alcoholic drinks being collectively known as booze, or grog. (With the exception of wine, which is known as 'plonk', 'steam', or 'bombo'.)

BOSS
Webster says that the word 'boss' comes from the Dutch *baas*, meaning master. But many Australians who have trouble with bosses would prefer Webster's geological definition — 'A protuberant, domelike, mass of igneous rock, congealed beneath the surface and laid bare by erosion.'

This would apply particularly to "bald-headed bosses'.

There is constant warfare in Australia — declared or undeclared — between the 'boss' and the 'worker'.

Most bosses are 'orright when you get to know 'em'. But it is not easy to get to know 'em.

In England, bosses are called 'sir', when directly addressed. But Australians don't like the word 'sir'. They prefer 'boss'. Or 'chief'.

If he's 'a good boss', Aussies will use his Christian name. If he's 'a crook boss' they will be completely impersonal, and avoid giving him any title at all. Except, after he's walked away, to mutter 'bastard' — and mean it.

The word 'boss' is also often used as a general term of address for people who are not bosses.

'G'day, boss, how ya doin'?' —

'What time does the next train go, boss?' —

Or when introducing the wife — 'Meet the boss.'

If you hear a man described as being 'a bossy bastard', he'll be one who 'throws his weight about'

And if you hear one described as being 'the boss cocky', he'll be the real boss — the 'top dog'.

BOT

Anyone who lives by constantly 'putting the bite on' others is a 'bot'.

'Bots' are allergic to work, and impervious to insult, and although they have no visible means of support, are nearly always drunk.

They have the remarkable ability — a magical and inexplicable ability — to disappear instantly ten seconds before the arrival of policemen.

BOTTLER

A 'bottler' is not one who succeeds in bottling a bot; nor is it a bot with access to more bottles than most of the breed.

'Bottlers' are the complete opposite of bots. They are worthy of very high praise; they could be successful jockeys, or football players.

He who performs well, and earns money for his backers, is indeed a 'bottler'.

And he who renders you superb personal service, over and above the call of duty, is that prince — that peer of peers — the 'little bottler'.

Supposing the temperature is well over 100 degrees F., and your thirst is fierce, and it's too hot to go 'up to the pub', and a friend arrives with clinking ice-cold dew-wet bottles of your favourite brew. There is no better way to express your feelings of surprise, gratitude. elation, and restored belief in the essential goodness of humanity than by a sincere and heartfelt, 'You little bottler, Bertie—you bloody little bottler.'

BUCKJUMPER

An untamed and untameable horse, who does his best to unseat his rider, is one form of 'buckjumper'.

Another is an undigested and indigestible item of food, cooked in the outback. — Take one frypan; grease liberally with mutton-fat; pour in a mixture of flour, water and salt; cook on both sides until brown; spread with jam, and start chewing.

This type of buckjumper, when eventually swallowed, is guaranteed to weigh heavily enough in a man's stomach to secure him a permanent seat on the back of any 'buckjumper' of the other type.

BUGGER

As a noun, this can be an alternative for 'bastard'. A bastard can be 'a bit of a bugger', and vice versa.

But as a verb, it has various meanings, most frequently in the sense of 'wrecking the system'.

'She was a good little pub until that new bloke took over, an' buggered it up.'

As noun or verb, it is not usually used by — or in the presence of — ladies.

There exists also an unidentifiable place called 'buggery'. No one knows where it is. But if you annoy an Australian, he is likely to suggest that you go there.

BUSH
The country. Anywhere outside of cities.

When a man says he's 'bushed', it does not mean that he is tired — it means that he is lost. It is possible for a 'bushie' to be bushed in a city, and for a 'city slicker' to be bushed in the bush.

If you 'get bushed' in a city, consult a policeman. If you get bushed in the bush, sit down and wait. Somebody will probably find you before you become breakfast for crows, hawks, eagles, and ants.

B*B*B*B*B*B*B

26

CHUCK

'There's a keg on tonight — we're all chuckin' in.'

This will be an invitation to a party, the central attraction of which will be a keg of beer; and all males present will contribute to its cost.

Any group expenses can be shared by individuals 'chucking in'.

And any individual has the right to 'chuck in' his job, by resigning — or 'tellin' the boss what do with it'.

'Chuck' is also the verb to throw. But a peculiarity of its imperative mood is that the personal pronoun 'me' never follows it. You don't chuck 'me' anything — you always 'chuck us'.

'Chuck us that spanner, Joe.'

If the spanner is broken beyond repair, it is 'chucked out'. But the one who chucks it out is not a 'chucker out'. A 'chucker out' chucks out undesirables from places of public entertainment.

The 'cellarman' in a pub is usually a big bloke, because he has to handle heavy kegs of beer, and double as a 'chucker out'.

CLOUT

A 'clout on the ear hole' is a 'belt in the lug'. To 'clout' a man is to hit him — or 'dong him', or 'drop him', or 'belt him one', or 'put him on the knuckle'. But you don't clout him 'down'. To 'clout down' is to enforce discontinuance of a pleasurable activity — generally illegal.

'We were goin' all right until the cops clouted down on us.' —

'Used to be able to get a drink here after hours, but the sergeant clouted down on it.'

But to 'clout on' is different. You shouldn't 'clout on' anything that does not belong to you. That's stealing.

CONK

A 'bugle' — a 'beak' — a nose. And anything 'on the conk', or 'on the bugle', or 'on the beak', or 'on the nose' has deteriorated, gone bad, stinks, and should be thrown out.

By inference, you can also 'conk' a man by hitting him.

But 'conk out' has an entirely different meaning. When you 'conk out', you're exhausted; you've had it; you're dead.

Engines can conk out too; and TV sets—and marriages.

COOT

Bloke of inferior quality. Generally used in the third person, and prefaced by adjectives such as 'silly', or 'stupid', or 'wall-eyed', or 'bald-headed', etc.

COP

A policeman. Also known as a 'walloper', a 'John hop', or a 'John'.

If addressing policemen directly — asking them, for example, the way to such and such a place, person or thing — the correct terms are 'constable' or 'sergeant'. 'Mug cop' is dangerous.

COW

Old-timers will tell you that Australia is the only country in the world where a dark horse can be a fair cow. That's when he wins, and nobody has backed him.

Although the phrase 'fair cow' is now seldom heard, 'cow' is still current. Anything refractory, unpredictable, exasperating, can be 'a cow of a thing'. If it's blowing a gale, raining sideways, and is 'cold enough to freeze 'em off a brass monkey', it could be 'a cow of a day'.

It is difficult to understand why the productive, contemplative, philosophical, harmless cow should have become a symbol for the things that irritate her master. Perhaps the reason lies in the same inverted thinking that causes Australians to address a tall man as 'shorty', or 'tich', and a little bloke as 'lofty'.

CROOK

No good. Sick.

'Things are crook.' 'I'm crook.' 'The weather's crook.' 'That bloody beer's crook.'

But 'She went crook on me' means she abused me.

And 'I'm crooked on her' means I don't like her any more. (Probably because she went crook on me.)

CUT

Your share of anything. If invited to 'get in for your cut', it is advisable to get in for it. Otherwise you are likely to 'miss out'. In which case you'll be as 'silly as a cut snake'.

But if you 'go crook' about it, you'll be told to 'cut it out'. Which will mean 'shut up and behave yourself'.

C*C*C*C*C*C*C

D

DAG
The bloke who likes practical jokes is 'a bit of a dag'.

The lump of dried excreta hanging behind a sheep is also a 'dag'.

Both should be removed.

DAMPER
Take the recipe as for 'buckjumpers', but use self-raising flour, or plain flour with the addition of baking powder. Place in oven, camp oven, or the ashes of a camp fire.

The result will not resemble bread, but it will be a substitute. Eat it with corn beef, and wash it down with strong hot tea.

Not for delicate stomachs.

Also — to 'put a damper on' any proposed activity is to discourage it.

DEAD
This little word has many idiomatic uses. Some examples:

'You're a dead ringer for your brother' — you resemble him.

'He's a dead cert' — he can't lose. (Although he generally does.)

'The bastard ran dead' — he was not trying to win.

'Do that an' you're a dead duck' — the result will be disastrous.

'He got me dead' — he caught me in the act.

'Dead as a door-nail' — dead indeed, and ready for burial.

'Dead to the world' — sound asleep.

'I'm not dead nuts on that feller' — I don't like him very much.

'Dead head' — a useless character; a passenger.

'He was dead on his feet' — he was exhausted.

'Dead spittin' image' — an exact replica.

'He was playin' dead' — he was waiting for an opportunity.

'Dead an' won't lie down' — dumb; stupid.

'Dead marine' — an empty bottle.

'She's a dead town today' — there's nobody about.

And if you're 'dead beat', you're very tired.

But if you are referred to as a 'dead-beat', you will be the equivalent of a bot, and of no further use to society.

DEKKO
A look.

'Have a dekko at this.' —

'They're doin' a good job on that new house o' Smithy's — I had a dekko at it this arvo.' —

'You don't believe me? All right, go an' have a dekko yourself.'

DEMON
A plain-clothes policeman. A detective.
Demons have poker faces, cold eyes, and wear hats.

DILL
A bloke whose intentions are good, and whose demeanour is amiable — but who lacks intelligence, and is therefore hard to talk to, with, or at. A dill is only 'eighteen bob in the pound', or is 'short of a shingle', or 'has a screw loose', or is 'not right in the skull'.
'Nits', 'nuts', and 'nongs' are all dills.

DINGO
The native Australian wild dog — a menace to pastoralists, to be trapped, shot, or poisoned at every opportunity; an animal detested by all, with a bounty on his head.
Consequently, any cowardly human, who refuses to face his responsibilities or his opponents, is a 'dingo'.
The word is also used as a verb — 'So I fronted the bastard, but he dingoed on it, and backed down.'

DINKUM
The real, the true, and the honest. 'Dinkum blokes', 'dinkum Aussies', and 'fair dinkum' statements cannot be faulted.
Anybody or anything 'not fair dinkum' is false.

DIRTY
'He came the dirty on me' — he used unfair tactics; he 'put in the dirt'.

And the word is used in a peculiar way to qualify, and increase the effectiveness of, the adjective 'big'.

'I'm just turnin' the corner, and there's this dirty big truck.' —

'Sittin' there mindin' our own business, and up comes this dirty big cop.'

DOB IN
Australians are noted for a deep-seated reluctance to report any fellow-citizen to anyone in a position of authority. Police, bosses, foremen, wives, etc. must do their own detecting.

Anybody who 'dobs in' anybody else is a 'bastard' — in the worst sense of the term.

DODGER
Bread. 'Chuck us a hunk o' dodger, will ya?' should be translated 'Would you mind passing me a slice of bread, please?'

In the bush, a 'poddy-dodger' is a calf-thief.

DONE
If you are overcharged for anything, you've 'been done'.

But a threat to 'do' a man is not a threat to overcharge him. It's a threat of physical annihilation — often made at a 'do', which is a party.

DRONGO
Anyone so deficient in character and ability as to be called a drongo could be classified as unfit for human society.

But drongoes — like the 'bludgers' they resemble — are rare.

DRUM

There are many kinds of drums — 4-gallon drums, 44-gallon drums, bass drums, side drums, kettle drums, etc.— as well as people who are 'not worth a drum', and commercial travellers 'drummin' up' trade.

There's the horse who 'never ran a drum' because he was last in the race.

And there's the true, fair dinkum information imparted to you by people who 'drum you', or 'give you the drum'.

So if you want the drum about anything, ask an expert.

DUD

No good. Anything that won't work.
    'Don't buy Bill's old bomb — she's a dud.'—
    'No, I didn't take that job — it was a dud.' —
    'How'd you go with that dame last night?'
    'No good — she was a dud.'

DUMP

Functional objects that refuse to function are 'duds'. But inanimate objects with little to recommend them, such as inferior pubs, clubs and places, are 'dumps'.
    'Aw, you don't want to go there, mate; that's a dump.'
As a verb, 'dump' means to dispose of.
    'That thing's a dud, son; take it out an' dump it.' —
    'I was all set to go for her in a big way, but she dumped me.'

If you go surfing, and you're an inexperienced surfer, you are likely to be picked up by a 'dumper' — a hollow-faced wave — and 'dumped'. This is an undignified experience. It also hurts.

DYKE

A toilet. Also known as a 'dunny', a 'shouse', a 'toot'. A place in which to 'spend a penny', or to 'pay a visit', or to 'kill a snake'.

The practice of 'kangarooing the dyke' — squatting on it with your feet on the seat — is reprehensible, and frowned upon by all purveyors of public amenities.

D*D*D*D*D*D*D*D

EARBASHER

Also known as a 'lug punisher'. The fellow who backs you into a corner, and talks and talks and talks and talks and talks.

Professional earbashers can be found in local government and parliamentary circles, where they spend most of their time earbashing each other, and annoy us less than the amateurs. Amateurs are to be avoided. Go to another pub.

EASY

'How's about we give this dump away, an' go round to Ryan's?'

'I'm easy' — I 'couldn't care less' either way; I'll do whatever you suggest.

'How would I go if I asked the boss for time off?'

'All right; he's easy.'

If you have a boss who's easy, you're 'on easy pickin's' — you have a comfortable job, with no problems.

EDGE

When somebody 'has the edge on you', he's just a little bit better than you are at whatever you happen to be doing. And if you happen to be backing race-horses, and you're not doing too well at it, the 'bookies' will have the edge on you.

But you can always 'edge out', and go home.

EGG

A verb of encouragement. To 'egg someone on' is to urge him to greater effort — or to persuade him to do something that you wouldn't do yourself.

But you would not 'egg on' a 'bad egg'. 'Bad eggs' have natural criminal and anti-social tendencies, and should not be encouraged.

EXTRA GROUSE

Beaut. Wonderful. Our beer is 'extra grouse'. So is the silence when there are no earbashers or lug punishers about.

E*E*E*E*E*E*E

FAIR GO

'Fair go, mate.' Or 'Give him a fair go.' A plea for sweet reasonableness and sportsmanship.

It is not a 'fair go' when visitors spend a few days or weeks in a place, and then appoint themselves authorities on it.

FANG

'Putting the bite on' somebody is also 'putting the fangs in'.

But anyone described as being 'good on the fang' will not be a perpetual borrower. If you're 'good on the fang' it will cost a lot to feed you.

FIZZLE

Things which fade gradually, and eventually cease to exist, can be said to 'fizzle out'.

Bushfires can fizzle out when there's nothing left to burn; jobs can fizzle out; love affairs can fizzle out.

FLIES

'Having one with the flies', or 'drinking with the flies' — a man standing alone at a bar, buying drinks for himself. Such a character is considered to be 'odd', or 'a bit off', or a 'snooty bastard' — a man who prefers flies to human beings.

But 'no flies on that feller' means 'that feller' is a very smart feller — shrewd, cunning, able to live just within the law.

FOUR-LETTER WORDS

Anglo-Saxon four-letter obscenities are the same wherever English is spoken. But in some countries there is more tolerance of them than there is in Australia. When an Australian drops a brick on his foot, or hits his thumb with a hammer, he is likely to produce one of these words; but there are few who use them in general conversation.

And it is considered extremely rude, crude and unforgivable to use any of them in the presence of women, who — presumably — have never heard them.

FULL

The way you get if you drink too much. 'Full as an egg', 'full as a boot', 'full as a goog', 'full as the family pot', etc., all mean drunk. The best thing to do, if in that condition, is to find a bed and 'flake out'. And there are hundreds of remedies for the next morning's hangover — none of them much good.

F*F*F*F*F*F*F*F

GALAH

A grey-backed, pink-breasted inland parrot, gregarious and noisy, destructive and useless, and considered to be 'as silly as a square wheel'.

Any human beings who possess these characteristics — particularly drivers of vehicles other than your own — are 'galahs'.

Most human galahs are young. If their galah habits persist, they may graduate, and become dills, or nongs.

GET

You are entitled to feel insulted if you are requested to 'go an' get' something done to you. Because whatever word is used to follow 'get', it will be a word with biological and undignified implications.

You have a choice of reply. The conventional reply is, 'I have been, an' I liked it.' This is made by characters who don't take the injunction too seriously; who don't feel themselves to be too deeply insulted.

But if you *do* feel deeply insulted by the bloke who

41

tells you to 'go an' get so-an'-so'd', then you will 'get stuck into him' — either verbally, or with your fists.

GIBBER

A stone; a boulder. 'Gibber plains' are vast areas of flat, sun-baked country, treeless and waterless, and covered with stones. They occur 'out in the Centre'.

GIG

Pronounced with the 'g' hard as in 'gutzer'.

A gig is a 'bit of an idiot'. He is mostly young, noisy, something of an exhibitionist, indulges in horseplay, gives girls the slap-and-tickle treatment, and is not noted for his intelligence. If his idiocy is particularly well advanced, he can become a 'prize gig' — which is the highest rank a gig can hope to reach. 'Gig' is also heard sometimes in the sense of 'look'. For example, 'Have a gig at this.'

GINK

(Pronounced with the 'g' hard, as in 'get') : A bloke who's 'a bit of a galah'.

GO

In addition to 'fair go', this word is used in many other ways. For example, 'Dunno much about it, but I'll have a go at it.'

Footballers and cricketers who are not doing their best are exhorted to 'have a go'.

And you may be warned to 'watch out for that dog, mate — he'll go ya'.

If he does, you'll be entitled to 'go crook' on the dog's owner, using choice words of your own choosing.

42

And if you become tired of cities and people, you can always 'go bush' — before you 'go west'. When you've 'gone west', you will be dead.

(There are other ways to die. You can 'kick the bucket', or 'cash in your chips', or 'push up daisies', or simply 'keel over'.)

But if you're 'a bit gone', you're some kind of a nut.

GONE A MILLION

Caught. Copped. 'Not in the race to get out of it.'

Characters trapped into marriage; 'apprehended in the commission of a felony'; trying to sell 'hot' watches to demons; discovered in 'flagrant delicto' by husbands — all are 'gone a million'.

A classical illustration is cartoonist Emile Mercier's drawing of a very hairy yak standing in an illegal parking area. A 'brown bomber', peering under the mass of hair, says to the yak's owner, 'I don't care what you call it— if it's got wheels you're gone a million.'

GUTZER

When your carefully worked out plan falls through; when you don't get the taxation rebate you expected; when your tender for a job is accepted, and you lose money on the deal; when you back a 'stone moral cert', and he runs last; when you fall flat on your puss in the mud, and you're wearing your best 'bag of fruit' — you have, my friend, 'come a gutzer'.

G*G*G*G*G*G*G

HELL

'Go to hell.'

  'Eh? Like hell I will.'

  'Go on, get to hell out of here.'

  'Who the hell do you think you're talkin' to?'

  'I'm talkin' to you; now go on — hell off.'

  A useful word, 'hell'.

  'Where the hell do ya think you're goin'?'

  'What's it got to do with you?'

  'Hell, nothin'. I was just askin'. A man can be polite,
  can't he?' —

  'Who the hell was that?'

  'How the hell would I know? Never saw him before
  in me life.'

  'To hell with him, then.'

  'Yeah — to hell with him.'

The Aussie hell seems to be a very strange place. The
weather can be 'as hot as hell', 'as cold as hell', 'as windy
as hell', 'as dry as hell', 'as dusty as hell', or 'as wet as
hell'. Things can be 'as high as hell', or 'as low as hell'.

And you can go to a party and have 'a hell of a good time'.

If chased by a bull, you 'run like hell', and 'yell like hell', and wish the fence wasn't such 'a hell of a long way away'.

When your wife abuses you, she 'gives you hell', but most of the time she's 'a hell of a good sport'. Should she try to persuade you to buy her a new hat, 'she hasn't got a hope in hell'.

Sydney's 'a hell of a big town', but Sydneysiders think Melbourne is 'a hell of a place'.

You can take sides in the friendly rivalry between Sydney and Melbourne if you like — and 'a hell of a lot of good that will do you.'

HOOLY-DOOLY

An exclamation of surprise, or astonishment, or unbelief, when confronted by an incredible event, which your eyes see, but which your reason doubts. Or when told of such an event by a bloke who is not accustomed to 'draw the long bow', or to 'pull your leg'.

The publican shouts for everybody in the bar, and is completely sober at the time —

The horse that has 'run like a hairy goat' during the whole of his long racing career, never finishing nearer the money than second last, wins the Melbourne Cup by ten lengths —

A politician makes no promises, thinks his opponent is a better man than he is, and never makes a speech lasting longer than five minutes —

A motor-cycle cop races up alongside you when you're doing 50 in a 35-mile zone, says, 'Would you mind pulling over to the kerb, please, sir', gets in with you, admires your new car, whistles his appreciation when you tell him it will do a hundred, suggests a good stretch of road where you can 'let her out', and then takes you into the nearest pub and buys you a beer —

The boss sends for you, acknowledges the fact that you are one of the lowest-paid of all the employees, states that he has had his eye on you for some time and is impressed by your remarkable qualities, and asks if you would, as a personal favour to him, take over the management of the business during his six months' long-service leave —

The Sydney Opera House is finished, paid for, costs less than originally estimated, is officially opened, functions perfectly, has unlimited parking space, has 'house full' signs out every night, and is making an enormous profit—

'Hooly-dooly.'

H*H*H*H*H*H*H

ICKY

An adjective — sticky; dicey. A situation where the wrong decision could lead to disaster.

If you forgetfully make a date with two different women, for the same place at the same time on the same night, the situation could be described as 'icky'.

IN IT

'Will you be in it?' 'Go on, be in it.' 'Goin' fishin' next Saturday — be in it?' 'He wanted to turn on a blue, but I wouldn't be in it.'

The 'it' that you may be asked to be 'in' could be anything done in company with others. But it's generally either physically or alcoholically exhausting, or both. So before you decide to be in it, have a good look at it.

IT

Here we digress for a moment, to discuss some of the peculiarities of the Australian accent.

47

Very few Australians pronounce 'it' as 'it'. If you listen to the average Englishman saying 'it', you will hear him pronounce the word with a short and distinct 'i'. But none of the vowels in the Roman alphabet can phonetically reproduce the Australian sound. The Aussie rendering of the 'i' in 'it' is atonic — a kind of toneless grunt.

The same sound occurs in the Malay language, and Anglicized Malay renders it by inventing a toneless vowel, written 'ĕ'. Perhaps a grunted 'uh' would come fairly close.

But we can hardly write 'uht'; and in writing Australian dialogue the author has, in the past, compromised with 'ut'. This is a poor compromise, but is nearer the Australian sound than 'it'. If we had the vowel 'ĕ', the problem would be solved.

Similar difficulties arise with the pronouns 'he', 'she' and 'me'. But no compromise is possible here. The 'e' in these words is a diphthong — an 'er' sound, followed by the 'e' sound. 'Mĕe', or 'mei' would give it — if we had 'ĕ'. But we haven't. And Americans and English, who pronounce the 'e' in 'he', 'she' and 'me' as a pure sound — similar to the Italian 'i' — will just have to imagine the Australian sound, when they see these words written.

Of the other vowels, 'a' is long in words like 'class', 'glass', 'pass', etc. — we've already mentioned 'ass' — and short in most other cases. Some characters make it long in 'dance', 'chance' and 'plant' — but these pronunciations are regarded as affectations.

The pronoun 'I' will be heard as anything from 'Oi' to 'Ai'.

'O' does not have the American or Continental 'aw'

value, but is a diphthong, pronounced as though preceded by a broad 'a'.

And the sound of 'u' varies from 'oo' to 'ew'. 'Duty', for example, is not 'dooty', but 'dewty'.

And if your ears tell you that a bloke says, 'She's good to die', don't think he's advocating suicide. He'll mean 'she's good today' — probably referring to the quality of the beer, the weather, or the state of his wife's health.

Anyway, if our vowel sounds 'stump' you, don't blame mee. Ut's hard to explain 'em, an' Oi'm doin' ut the best way Ai can.

ITIE

Pronounced 'eye-tie'. An Italian. There are a lot of Italians in Australia, and generally speaking they're not bad blokes. They're 'always laughin' ', and their young women are 'easy on the eyes'.

Early Italian migrants — and Greeks — were known as 'dagoes'; but the word has an offensive meaning now, and is seldom used. Ities are sometimes called 'dings', which is a reasonably friendly word. If you hear of one referred to as a 'dago bastard', the character using the phrase is likely to be 'a bit of a bastard' himself.

Ities eat spaghetti and drink plonk. But they also like to eat steak and drink beer, and are therefore 'decent blokes'.

I*I*I*I*I*I*I

JACK

In its various forms — John, Jean, Johann, Giovanni, etc.
— probably one of the most common of Christian names
amongst people of European descent. Common in Australia, too. But 'jack up' does not mean that Jack is a ball
player who is about to face the pitcher. When Jack 'jacks
up', he refuses to co-operate.

'An' this galah — me boss, I mean — wants me to
work through me lunch hour. So I jack up. Wouldn't you?'
(He probably 'got jack' of the job, too, and told the boss
what to do with it.)

In Australia, as in other countries, there are a few
selfish blokes about who live by the 'Jack principle'—
their philosophy being, 'Bugger you, Jack, I'm all right.'

JACKEROO

A young learner on a sheep or cattle station. Allegedly
in training for management. Eats with the boss. Expected

to do a maximum amount of work for a minimum of salary. His status is similar to that of a midshipman in the Navy — neither a seaman nor an officer, and generally abused by both.

Jackeroos 'from the city' learn the hard way. They are on the receiving end of all the old bush practical jokes, and need to have placid dispositions to survive.

Jackeroos may be called many things by shearers, station hands, stockmen, and bosses, but the properties on which they work and suffer are always called 'stations' — never 'ranches'.

The author once heard a jackeroo describe his boss as a 'dirty rotten lousy up-jumped never-come-down product of a misalliance between a rabid sea-serpent and a half-caste sailor's crossbred mangy mongrel of a bloody dog.'

A well-spoken opinion. The boss's opinion of the jackeroo is not known.

J*J*J*J*J*J*J

KACK

Luck—but never good.

'Put me lunch down—went to me coat to get me matches — come back, an' there's this mongrel dog that's been hangin' around the last week knockin' off me sandwiches.'

A sympathetic rejoinder to this tragic tale would be— 'Hard kack.'

The word was at one time a euphemism for excreta, but is now very seldom heard in this sense.

KICK

If you are asked to 'kick in' for a party, a wedding, a farewell to a workmate, a dead barmaid, a raffle — for anything — you are being asked to contribute coin of the realm, according to the state of your 'kick'. If you are broke, you will be excused. But if you have 'dough in the kick', kick in.

And 'kick the tin', too, when it's your turn to buy a round of drinks. If you won't put your hand in your pocket, you have 'death adders in your kick', and are afraid of being bitten. Characters with death adders in their kicks are 'lousy bastards'.

KIP

You stand in the middle of a ring of men. You have two pennies. There is money at your feet. The ring-keeper invites a bettor or bettors to 'cover' it. He invites others to 'get set on the side', and side-bets are made. When you throw the pennies in the air, will they 'come down heads', or will you 'throw tails'? You are known as the 'spinner'.

You toss the spinning coins, and down they come, and some men shout with joy, and others curse.

The flat strip of wood on which you arrange the coins before tossing them is called a 'kip'.

The game itself is called 'two-up'. It is played in all States. It is illegal.

In the courts, it is always given the quaint old name of 'heading 'em'. Which amuses two-up players, spinners, and ring-keepers, even as they are paying their fines.

If you stay up until dawn playing two-up, you will become very sleepy and will be pleased to go to your 'kip' — which is bunk, or bed.

The word also doubles for 'sleep'; so that when you reach your bunk, you can 'have a bit of a kip'.

KNOCK

Don't be horrified when somebody tells you he is 'knocked up'. It does not mean that he is pregnant. It means that he is tired. Ladies become knocked up by too much housework or dancing. You may use the phrase anywhere, any time, in any company.

But don't be a 'knocker'. Knockers are people who deride all things and projects, and thereby destroy enthusiasm.

And don't 'knock anything off' either. To knock something off is to steal it, thereby getting yourself into trouble with employers, cops, wallopers, demons and/or your neighbours.

You are, however, entitled to 'knock off'. To knock off is to cease work for the day. It's the most pleasant of all the 'knocks'.

K*K*K*K*K*K*K

LAIR

A lout — over-dressed, under-mannered, noisy and obnoxious. Generally referred to as a 'mug lair'.

To 'lair up' is to over-dress yourself, or alternatively to enjoy yourself in a crude and noisy way.

Lairs and 'lairisers' are regarded as public nuisances. They are mostly young. There are not many of them.

LASH

Sometimes this word is spelt with a 'b', and pronounced 'bash'. But if 'bash' is used the way 'lash' is used, it will mean what 'lash' means. And 'lash' means 'go'. Not the 'go' in 'go on', or 'go away', or 'go an' get —', but the 'go' in 'all right, I'll have a go', implying lack of experience in the situation, making no promises of success, but expressing willingness to try.

'See where a bloke ate fifteen dozen oysters. Reckon you could eat that many?'

'Dunno. But I wouldn't mind havin' a lash at 'em.'

Willingness to have a 'lash' — or a 'bash' — at anything not previously attempted, will earn you admiration from a race of people to whom having a 'lash' at anything — including you — is almost a way of life.

LEMONY
'Is that an orange or a lemon?'

'Suck it an' see.'

If it's a lemon, the sucker's face will register repugnance, as though having eaten of the 'acid of discontent'.

The expression is sometimes seen on the faces of wives who have not been sucking lemons, but who have been thinking of the deficiencies in the characters of their husbands.

Such thoughts, apart from producing discontented faces, generally breed reproving words.

'How did your missus treat you when you got home last night?'

'Went lemony on me.'

LOAF
The verb to do nothing.

'Just loafing' is a good way to spend a holiday. Permanent loafers, however, are not respected. They're little better than 'bludgers'.

A certain amount of 'loafing on the boss's time' is possible, but to get away with it you have to use your 'loaf' — which is your head.

LOUSY
A frequently used and opprobrious adjective, applied to certain forms of 'bastards', and many types of things.

56

People with death adders in their kicks, the Government, numerous bosses, the weather, the state of the roads — anything or anybody can be 'lousy'.

You can also 'feel lousy', if you're 'feeling crook'.

'An' I come home, an' what's me missus got for lunch? A lousy tin o' sardines.'

LURK

Short cuts to success, easy ways of doing things, methods of defeating laws and regulations, schemes for doing work of your own in your employer's time, etc., are known as 'lurks'. One who is proficient at profiting by such back-door activities is a 'lurk merchant'. He 'knows all the lurks'.

A 'good lurk' is any quick and easy way of overcoming a difficulty. Should you, by some subterfuge, succeed in extracting from your employer more money for less work, that would be 'an extra good lurk'.

L∗L∗L∗L∗L∗L∗L

MAD

Like the word 'bastard', the word 'mad' in Australia very rarely expresses its dictionary meaning.

'Who's your mad mate?' does not mean that your mate is insane. It is a friendly reference to your own eccentricity, implying that any mate of yours must necessarily be a little 'odd' — but odd in a praiseworthy way.

'Went fishin' with me mad mate.' —

'We'll have a couple o' beers — an' give us one for me mad mate; she's out in the car.'

If you are, however, extremely eccentric, you would be 'mad as a meataxe', or 'mad as a cut snake'. But not insane. Not a 'candidate for the loony bin'. Such candidates are said to have 'gone off their heads', or 'gone off their rockers'.

But if you 'get mad', you will not have gone off your head or rocker. You will be angry.

And if you disappear somewhere 'the other side of the black stump', or 'west of the rabbit-proof fence', and somebody asks, 'What happened to Bill?', the answer is likely to be, 'He went mad an' they shot him.' Which means, 'Haven't got a clue where he is, and couldn't care less.'

MANGY
A type of 'bastard'. Mean. Lousy. Has 'death adders in his kick'. Wouldn't shout for his mother if she was dyin' o' thirst.' 'Too lousy to put a penny in a blind man's tin.' 'Popular as a mangy dog.'

Mangy bastards should not visit pubs, clubs, or other people's homes. When they visit your home, they never bring 'a ticket to get in' — a bottle; they always drink yours.

Nevertheless, if you are *invited* to an Aussie home, don't bring a 'ticket'. Aussies like to dispense hospitality — once. After that you ought to 'kick in'. There will be protests, but they should be ignored. It is better to be known as a 'decent old bastard' than as a 'mangy old bastard'.

MATE
Your best friend. When your 'mate' is in trouble, you go to his assistance, no matter what he's done. A man must 'stick by his mates'.

The word is also used loosely as a general form of address for acquaintances and strangers. 'G'day, mate', 'How ya goin', mate?', 'Good on ya, mate', 'No, not now, mate', 'Righto, mate, be seein' ya', etc.

METHO
'On the metho.' 'A metho drinker.' A character who has sunk so low that he drinks methylated spirit, ignoring its

foul taste and lethal potential because of its high alcohol content and low price.

Members of the Methodist Church are also known as 'Methos', or 'Metho drinkers', although they don't drink metho, or in many cases any other kind of alcohol.

So if a bloke is introduced to you as a 'metho', take a good look at him. If he's thin, vague, glassy-eyed, unshaven, and 'smells like a brewery-horse's blurt', he'll be a genuine drinker of metho. If he looks normal, but takes only tea. coffee, or 'lolly water' (soft drinks), he's the other kind, and should be treated with respect.

MOB

'Mob o' sheep', 'mob o' cattle', 'mob o' goats', 'mob o' galahs', 'this mob', 'that mob'.

If your mob don't get on well with our mob, then there's something wrong with your mob, because our mob's a good mob. Not like that weird mob down in Melbourne. Or that mad mob up in Sydney.

Any group of living things with similar interests or peculiarities is a 'mob'. And if you want peace in life 'you gotta go with the mob'.

MUD

Anything 'up to mud' is 'not up to much'. It's no good. It's 'buggered'.

You'll be feeling 'up to mud' yourself, if you have a bad hangover — caused by raising your glass too often and saying, 'Mud in your eye', or 'Here's mud', or just briefly and simply 'Mud.'

If you do this too often, you will become very fat, and

will earn for yourself the title of 'mud-guts', or 'old mud-guts'.

In the building trade, 'mud' means mortar. Bricklayers' labourers have nightmares peopled by red-faced 'brickies' constantly screaming for 'more mud'.

MUG
A bloke who 'hasn't got a clue'. A beginner. A know-nothing. Also one who gets taken in — a sucker.

Drivers who do the wrong thing are referred to as 'mugs', or 'mug galahs'.

And there is a type of metal cup — plain or enamelled — used for drinking tea or coffee 'on the job', or 'in the bush', which is also called a mug. (Glass mugs are for beer.)

Your face is a 'mug', too. But don't worry about it. Most people with 'ugly mugs' have pleasant dispositions.

MY
An American recently asked the author, 'Why do so many Australians say me, when they mean my?' The author didn't know. He still doesn't know.

M*M*M*M*M*M*M

NED KELLY

Australia's most famous bushranger. Highwayman extraordinary, bank robber de-luxe, scourge of the Victorian police force. He was betrayed, wounded, captured, and hanged.

The same fate should overtake present-day 'robbers', all of whom are known as 'bloody Ned Kellys'.

Included in this Ned Kelly category are 'hungry' retailers, 'super' salesmen, proprietors of 'clip joints', characters who overcharge for mediocre work and services, and the bloke who sells you a second-hand, guaranteed, 'every bit as good as new and cheap as dirt' vehicle, which falls to pieces in the first hundred miles.

If caught by one of these types, you will be justified in exclaiming loudly, for all to hear, 'Who said bloody Ned Kelly was dead?'

To say that a man is 'as game as Ned Kelly', on the other hand, is to praise him highly. It means that he has 'real guts'— is brave to the point of recklessness in the face of any odds.

NIGGLY
Irritable. Bad-tempered.

'Leave him alone, mate — he's niggly this morning.'

NIT
Apart from being a synonym for a 'nong', or a 'nut', or a 'dill', the word has another meaning. To 'keep nit' is to watch out for the approach of authority. 'Nit-keepers' are essential for those engaged in any illegal activity.

Nit-keepers are also known as 'cockatoos', the native white cockatoo being a bird that screams at the approach of potential enemies.

(Note: Buy some insecticide if you find nits in your hair. They'll hatch out to become lice.)

N*N*N*N*N*N*N

OFF

When the beer's 'off', you wait for it to come on again; when the meat's 'off', you throw it away, because it will be bad; when you 'go off', you'll be getting married; when you 'blow off', you'll be abusing somebody; and when you 'piss off', you'll be leaving. (Which you may be asked to do if you tell a story that's 'a bit off'.)

OIL

'Oil' is roughly equivalent to 'drum'. When you are 'given the oil', or 'the good oil', or 'the dinkum oil', you are receiving correct information.

But as a verb, 'oil' differs from 'drum' in that it is always followed by 'up'. You can 'drum' a bloke directly, but you can't 'oil' him. You have to 'oil him up'.

'Did you get the drum about what's on on Sunday?'
'Yeah. Joe oiled me up.'

ON

When anything is about to function, predictably or unexpectedly, it is said to be 'on'. Should bad weather make the holding of a race meeting doubtful, and then a late clearance make it possible, it will be announced that 'the races are on'. All sporting activities can be 'on' in this way.

But: 'Joe still on with dame?'

'No, that's off. He's on with another one now.'

And when a bloke 'makes an exhibition of himself', by eccentricity either of dress or behaviour, attention is likely to be drawn to him with the phrase, 'Be on him, will ya?'

Which is a different kind of 'on' to being 'on' a horse. When you're on a horse, you've backed him to win.

And if he wins, you'll be congratulated with 'Good *on* ya.'

OODLES

Plenty.

'Righto, mate — we'll be there about eight o'clock. Want me to bring any grog?'

'Gees, no — we got oodles.'

With the letter 'b' in front of it, this strange little word means money. So 'oodles of boodle' equals 'plenty moolah' — or 'no shortage of oscar' — or 'lashin's of splosh'.

OPEN SLATHER

That unusual situation, or special occasion, where the forces of law and order turn blind eyes and deaf ears to communal infringement of Regulations.

'If you're goin' out that way, call in at So-an-so's pub. She's open slather there on Sundays.' —

'Aw, don't tell me there's no gambling in Broken Hill. I've been there, mate — it's open slather.'

OVER

'Blue', or 'off', stories in mixed company are 'over the odds', or 'over the fence'.

To 'bowl a bloke over', or 'do him over', is to fight him and beat him. So if you 'get done over' you'll be very unhappy for a few days, but the bloke who did it may soon 'come over', and be friendly again.

O*O*O*O*O*O*O

PERK

If you want your share of perks,
Learn the ropes, and all the lurks.

'Perks' are the little extras that you get out of your job, over and above the normal pay and amenities. They make life more pleasant.

There is, however, another kind of 'perk'; and if you are ever fortunate enough to go cruising amongst the Barrier Reef islands, and you want to make friends with deck-hands, you should know how to do this one properly. You'll know when you're going to do it. First you start yawning — more than usual, even if you're naturally a sleepy type — then you feel cold perspiration breaking out on your forehead. You will then just have time to take out your false teeth, wet your finger, hold it up to find out which way the wind is blowing, and crawl over other bodies to the lee side of the ship.

Never, never, never, perk into the wind. Deck-hands don't mind the stuff going all over you, but they object to it going all over the ship. They have to clean it up. And be sure to keep your hands out of it — it leaves permanent finger-marks on the rails.

If you happen to drink too much beer ashore, and feel like 'perking', the floor of the bar is not the place. Stagger to the toilet.

PESTER

A verb derived from 'pest'. Pests are things like insects, noxious weeds, rabbits, kangaroos, snakes, flying foxes, ticks, and certain human beings such as 'earbashers', and 'bots'. But the verb is applied only to humans.

Mum to the kids: 'Why don't you go out and play, and stop pestering me?'

Dad to his neighbour: 'There's only two ways to get rid of insurance salesmen — buy insurance or boot 'em out. They'll pester you for weeks if you don't.'

PISSANT

Courageous little men, or small dogs with lots of fight in them, are 'game as pissants'. To be classified 'game as a pissant' is to be praised very highly indeed.

Exactly what kind of an ant a pissant is, nobody seems to know. But he appears to be a fine fighting little ant, with 'a ton o' guts — game as Ned Kelly'.

POMMY

Or its abbreviation 'Pom'. An Englishman.

The true origin of this word is unknown. Because Englishmen have complexions like pomegranates is one theory. Because English convicts bore on their backs the letters P.O.H.M. — Prisoner of His Majesty — is another.

The title was originally derisive, but is now sometimes bestowed affectionately. A bloke can have a 'Pommy bastard' for a mate.

Nevertheless, a cultured English accent, to most Australians, indicates that the user is 'bungin' it on'. And a man accused of 'talkin' like a Pom' will indignantly deny it. Unless he likes Poms generally. Some do.

Americans are never called Poms. They're just 'bloody Yanks'.

POOPED

In the old days of sailing ships, a wave over the poop deck meant disaster. And this is probably the origin of the American word 'pooped', meaning 'exhausted'; 'had it'.

But Americans should know that when an Australian hears this word, he is first shocked, and then amused.

Most Aussies have forgotten about sailing ships, but the word 'poop' is remembered. It means excreta.

In this country, it is better for an American to forget about being 'pooped', and to become 'knocked up' instead.

PUB

Any hotel.

The primary purpose of a pub is to provide beer for the public. Its 'public bar' is patronized exclusively by males, who talk and smoke while they're drinking beer, the volume of sound increasing after each 'round', with more and more talkers, and fewer listeners. 'Yarns' are told — some of them clean; worries and inhibitions are forgotten; and the walls rock with the noise of 'skiting' (boasting)

and ribald laughter. 'Barmaids' scurry up and down, pour-
ing and serving the amber fluid, and calling everyone
'dear', or 'love'. And it is unusual to find anybody sitting
down.

The pleasures of the 'public bar' are sampled standing
up, ankle-deep in spilt beer, cigarette butts, and sundry
assorted discarded packages and wrappings, such as news-
papers from which the 'fish 'n chips' have been removed
and eaten.

A bloke with a large wide broom sometimes comes
through, and patrons are requested to 'move your feet,
please, gents'.

The 'saloon' — or private — bar is provided with
stools, and characters have been known to sit on them.

Every pub has a 'saloon bar', which is not so starkly
functional as the 'public'. There will be mirrors, orna-
ments, arrays of assorted bottles, better floor coverings,
and even flowers. The patrons will be mainly business and
professional men, talking 'shop', and being less noisy
about it. They will be paying a little more for their beer
and spirits

Drinkers of Scotch are mainly found in saloon bars.
And there is a tendency for women to infiltrate, but they
have not yet reached 'pest' proportions.

The proper place for women in any pub is the 'lounge'.
Here they sit at tables, with or without male escort, drink
their beer, and discuss the things women discuss when they
get together.

All pubs are required by law to provide accommodation
and meals. Most publicans consider this law to be a
nuisance, but some people take advantage of it, and eat
and sleep in pubs.

Pubs are faced with severe competition from clubs, which provide grog for members and visitors, but are not required to provide beds.

In the 'accommodation and meals' department, pubs must also compete with motels, whose numbers are rapidly increasing.

But the Aussie loves his pub, and to date, very few have 'gone broke'.

PUNT

To 'take a punt at' anything is the equivalent of to 'have a go'. But 'punters' are people who bet on racehorses. Punters are mugs.

P*P*P*P*P*P*P

QUACK

A doctor of medicine. Originally an unqualified, unregistered, unlicensed medical practitioner, using psychology and salesmanship in lieu of knowledge. But today — all doctors and surgeons.

'Aw well, see, me old man's off crook this week, so he's mindin' the kids, an' that gives me a chance to get out.'

'What's wrong with him? Did you have to get the quack in?'

'Yes, love. He only had the 'flu, but I had to get the quack so he could get a medical certificate to take to work.'

QUEEN

A 'queer', a 'pansy', a 'poofter', a 'ponce'. A male homosexual. Known to be 'camp'. 'Camp as a row o' tents.'

Queens are tolerated, provided they keep their perversions to themselves. The average Australian attitude is 'You can't help feelin' sorry for the poor bastards.' (Incidentally, the name 'Poncy Ponce' is hilarious to Australians.)

72

RATBAG

You drive at 50 mph in a 35 limit zone, and at 25 mph on an unrestricted highway —

You like to drink beer laced with sweet sherry —

Your favourite lunch is whisky and cake —

You wear a heavy suit with a tie when the thermometer registers 'over a hundred in the water bag' —

You surf outside the flags, in an area reserved for board riders —

You thumb your nose at all policemen, and call them 'mug cops' —

You walk bare-footed in country infested by snakes —

You don't like dogs, horses, or women —

You expect taxi-drivers, bus-conductors, and drink-waiters to call you 'sir' —

You are a 'ratbag'.

Anybody who behaves illogically or foolishly — or who disagrees with you on any subject — is a ratbag.

RAW PRAWN

'Want to buy a watch? Eighteen carat gold, seventeen jewels, genuine Swiss — cheap — just off a ship.'

'Aw, don't come the raw prawn, mate — go an' find another mug.'

If you succeed in 'conning' an Australian — if you make a 'sucker' of him — he'll curse and swear, but there'll be a certain amount of appreciation, even admiration, in his language.

'You wouldn't want to know — that little bloke with the glasses, you'd think butter wouldn't melt in his mouth — cunnin' little bastard put one over me.'

But if you lack finesse — if your attempt to deceive is transparent — then you are 'coming the raw prawn'. And you will be despised for your inept, stupid, and insulting appraisal of the mental calibre of your intended victim.

RED NED

The best of Australian wines are as good as any in the world. And this is not an empty boast; try them, and prove it for yourself.

The 'rough' Australian wines, which you can buy in bulk, and which are quite cheap, are better than their equivalents in France, Spain, Italy, etc.

Bulk claret — no vineyard or year of manufacture mentioned — is 'red ned'.

RING IN

To deceive by substitution. A good racehorse disguised as a poor one is a 'ring in'. Or is said to have been 'rung in'. It happens with footballers, too. And other things.

RINGER

A bush word, with two meanings.

The fastest shearer in a shearing shed — the shearer with the highest tally of sheep shorn — is the ringer for the shed.

In cattle country, however, a ringer is any stockman — any competent horseman who can do all the work expected of a stockman on a cattle station — as distinct from book-keepers, storemen, cooks, bosses, and other 'auxiliary' personnel.

But, of course, *never* jackeroos.

ROOT

Americans should be warned about this one. To 'root' for a favourite team, player, or performer, in the sense of lending encouragement, is not done in Australia. The Australian equivalent is to 'barrack' for. The word 'root' has a fundamental, biological, extremely vulgar application. And as a result of this meaning, the crudest, most direct, most unmistakable brush-off is to tell a man to 'go an' get rooted'. Insulting words, not to be used without due care and forethought.

On the other hand, 'rooted' can mean a deficiency in supplies. You can be 'rooted for bricks', 'rooted for beer', etc. But not when ladies are present.

ROTTEN

Drunk. 'Rotten with the grog.' 'Couldn't get any sense out of him — he was rotten.'

It is also used like 'lousy', the opposite of 'beaut'. Or combined with 'lousy'. 'Rotten weather', or 'rotten lousy weather', or 'lousy rotten weather', etc.

RUBBISH
To 'brush off'.

'What's the matter with old Jack? Said g'day to him this morning, an' he rubbished me.'

R*R*R*R*R*R*R

SACK

'I got the sack', or 'The boss sacked me' — my employment was terminated.

If I were an American, I would have been 'fired'.

But — 'I snatched me time' means 'I sacked myself'.

SCRUB

The natural growth on semi-arid land — not tall enough to qualify as trees. Mallee scrub, gidgee scrub, etc. And by inference, a synonym for 'the bush'; 'the cactus'.

'Dunno exactly where he lives — out in the scrub somewhere.'

As a verb, the word 'disposes' of people, and things.

'What happened to your mate?'

'He got on the booze, so I scrubbed him.' —

'We scrubbed that place last year; we never go there now.' —

'That knife's no good, mate. Scrub it, an' use this one.'

SEX

Like his religion — if any — sex to most Australians is a private and personal subject, and none of your business. The Aussie is seldom a frustrated character, and psychiatrists' couches are rare in the land. As one fellow said to the author, in a discussion on the high sex content of a lot of American literature, 'Who the hell wants to read about it?' Naturally there are a few voyeurs in the cities, as there are in all cities; but here they are few indeed. Typical of the general attitude would be this report, quoted verbatim:

'Tired? Man's got a right to be tired. We had our annual night out last night; all the blokes from work. Beaut dinner — not too many speeches — then out on the town. Snowy — you know Snowy — he says what say we go an' have a look at that strip-tease joint at the Cross? We're in the mood for anything, so in we go. The Pink Pussy Cat, they call it. Silly bloody name, ain't it? If you ever feel like goin' there, don't. All they got is bottled beer. Gives you a headache. I says to the waiter bloke, haven't you got any draught beer? No, he says. An' that's fair dinkum; they haven't. What you're s'posed to do at that joint is look at these sheilas gettin' undressed, an' drink bottled beer. Snowy's just as crooked on it as the rest of us. So we shot through, an' went back to the club. Extra good beer at the club. Got home at three o'clock. Snowy was full. I'll lay you tens he doesn't surface at all today.'

S.F.A.

Or Sweet F.A. Nothing. Nothing at all. 'Sweet Fanny Adams', is a polite translation. 'Bugger all' is a reasonably impolite alternative.

78

SHEILA

A young female. Also called a 'sort', a 'skirt', a 'dame', a 'doll', a 'charlie', a 'fabulous drop', a 'slashin' line', a 'bit o' homework', and many other things.

Any current British or American word or words applicable to young females will also be heard. And new terms of reference will be appreciated, if you have any, or care to invent any.

We're proud of our sheilas. You won't find 'better lookers' anywhere.

SHIRTY

Similar to 'lemony'. Except that you 'go' lemony, but you 'get' shirty.

'I didn't mean to offend him; I was just talkin', an' all of a sudden he got shirty.'

SHOOT THROUGH

To go away. To leave. An abridged version of 'shoot through like a Bondi tram', or 'shoot through on the Padre's bike', both of which are now extinct.

SHOUT

When you buy a drink for a man, you 'shout him one'. A group of convivial souls 'enjoyin' a few grogs' is a 'school', and members of a school 'shout' in rotation.

'No, it's my shout — you shouted last.'

If the publican shouts for you, he's either 'mad with the grog', or you're a V.I.P.

A publican's shout is a 'tomcat's delight' — 'one on the house'.

SKITE

Texans have a reputation for 'skiting', but a lot of Australians are good at it, too. To 'skite' is to boast, to 'belt a tin', to 'blow your own trumpet'.

Skites are not popular. You're entitled to debunk a skite. You do this by 'slinging off' at him.

SLOPS

Beer. Also called 'suds', and 'piss'.

'Good drop o' slops, this.' —

'You want to go to So-an-so's; extra good suds there.' —

'Bill? You won't see him today. He got on the piss last night.'

SMACKERS

Pounds. Not used in the singular.

'That bloody taxation mob — they all ought to be burnt. I worked it out I ought to get a rebate this year, an' what do they do? Hit me for two hundred smackers. Gettin' slugged for a couple o' hundred smackers is no joke, when you reckon you're in front.'

SPORT

A general term of address for a stranger, but not used as often as 'mate'. Whereas 'mate' is friendly, 'sport' indicates a certain amount of hostility towards the person addressed. 'Gunna have another one, mate?' as opposed to 'Listen, sport — you're bein' a bit of a bloody nuisance, aren't ya?' Which gives 'sport' three courses of action: (1) he can argue, and start a 'blue'; (2) he can 'piss off' and go somewhere else; or (3) he can 'square off' by apologizing, and correcting what may only be a misunderstanding.

In all its other uses, the word 'sport' is innocuous. You can play sport, follow sport, be a sport, or 'sport' a new tie or hat.

And a 'good sport' is anyone easy to get on with — a character, male or female, who will 'be in' anything.

SQUARE OFF

To apologize — verbally, or with a gift, or by voluntary labour.

'Squaring off' is any method of recompense for an offence committed against anybody's person or dignity.

'See you're out of the doghouse, mate.'

'Yeah. Squared off last night with a box o' chocolates.' —

'What've you done to Bill?'

'Dunno; have to go an' see him, an' square off.'

STAND OVER

All Australians object to being 'stood over'. They can be led, but not driven.

Anyone who issues orders, who tries to enforce obedience, is a 'standover merchant'. He is likely to 'get done over'.

Any attempt to 'stand over' waiters, waitresses, taxi-drivers — anybody — will bring disaster. Reasonable requests will always be granted; but orders, reasonable or unreasonable, will be resented. And retaliation, direct or indirect, will be inevitable.

If you earn a reputation for being a 'standover merchant', you've 'had it'.

STREWTH

If you get 'slugged for a couple o' hundred smackers', you're entitled to say 'Strewth'.

An exclamation. Equivalent to 'starve the crows', 'stiffen the lizards', 'stone the bloody dingoes', etc.

Standing alone, 'strewth' expresses horrified surprise. Incorporated in a sentence, it is mild, or even meaningless.

'Strewth, I dunno.' —

'Strewth, he didn't tell me.' —

'Strewth, look at the time — I gotta be goin'.'

S*S*S*S*S*S*S

THAT

English is the world's richest and most flexible language. It has been said that there is no thought conceivable by the mind of man which cannot be expressed in English. But the Aussies have one. Their idiomatic use of the little word 'that' defies description. Only by quoting examples can we get a clue to it:

'Now there's a jockey for you; the old Georgie.'

'Aw, don't gimme that; he's not that good.' —

'That's a big building they're puttin' up there.'

'You reckon? I don't think it's that big.' —

In another form — 'You should've seen her face when I told her. She was that excited.'

Also — 'What's in the tucker box, mate?'

'Aw, just bread an' meat an' that.'

If your first impression of Australia is unfavourable, wait a while until you get to know us. We're not that bad.

TOGS

Clothing. As 'working togs', 'swimming togs', etc.

The bloke wearing Sunday best is 'all togged up'.

TROT

You can be 'havin' a good trot', or 'havin' a bad trot', depending on 'how you're goin' '.

A run of bad luck is a 'bad trot', and vice versa.

Trotting races are known as 'the trots'. But if you've 'got the trots', or you have a 'touch of the trots', you're suffering from diarrhoea.

TUCKER

Food. There's 'good tucker', 'beaut tucker', 'bad tucker', 'lousy tucker', 'plenty tucker', 'lashin's of tucker', and 'not enough bloody tucker'. When there *is* enough tucker, you 'tuck in', or 'get stuck into it'.

Aussie tucker is all right. Wherever you go, you will be able to get the kind of tucker you like — provided you have some funds 'tucked away in your kick'. In private homes, you will find a meat dish of some sort is the main course. We're great meat eaters. Beef and lamb, mostly; pork sometimes; mutton seldom. (Except in sheep country, where lambs are too valuable to be eaten by their owners.)

You'll like our meat pies and sausages, too. 'Extra grouse tucker', they are.

And if you find yourself 'tuckered out', you won't be 'out of tucker'. You'll be 'knocked up' — or 'buggered'.

T*T*T*T*T*T*T

UP

There are many idiomatic uses for this little word, some of which have already been mentioned.

'Up the creek', 'up that certain creek', or 'buggered up' mean you're ruined, finished, all through.

'Up to putty', 'up to sh —', or just plain 'upter', mean no good; not 'up to scratch'.

'Up 'im' means fight him, 'get stuck into him', or 'declare him on' in an argument.

'Put up or shut up' is a command to back your statement or withdraw.

'He's up to something' — he's planning something, and we wonder what it is.

'What are you up to?' — what are you doing?

'What's up?' — what's wrong?

'What's up with you?' — why are you being so hard to get on with?

And if you're 'up a gumtree', you don't know how to handle a situation; you don't know what to do or say. So just 'belt up' — keep quiet and say nothing.

USUAL

Stay in this country long enough to sample all the brews, to find your favourite, to know the name of the size of glass you like, and you'll qualify as a 'resident' when you can walk into a bar and the barmaid says, 'What'll ut be— the usual?'

You'll qualify as a 'local' when you can walk into the bar, and have your 'usual' placed before you without anything being said. But when you want another one, don't ask for 'the same again'. Barmaids are linguistic purists. They'll remind you that you can't have 'the same', because you've already had it. They'll give you 'something similar'.

U*U*U*U*U*U*U

VAG
A vagrant; a person with 'no visible means of support'.

Vagrants are illegal in Australia. If you don't have independent means of support, you are supposed to work.

To be 'vagged' is to be arrested for vagrancy.

WALTZING MATILDA
'On the track'; 'on the wallaby'; 'carrying the swag'; 'humping the bluey'— wandering around the country with all your possessions on your back, looking for work and hoping you won't find it.

The late 'Banjo' Paterson wrote a ballad, which he called 'Waltzing Matilda'. It was set to music. Young 'professional' Australians, visiting other countries, like to sing it. It makes them feel superior, because nobody understands it. It is *not* the Australian national anthem.

WINGE

To whine, or complain. 'Winge-ers' are never satisfied.

'Aw, you don't want to take any notice of that bastard —he's always wingein'.'

WIPE

Similar to 'rubbish'.

'He wanted me to take a job with his mob, but I wiped him.' —

'*That* bastard; asked him for a loan of a couple o' smackers, an' he wiped me.'

WOG

Influenza. Or any allied disease.

'Tell him I can't come to work today; I got the wog.' —

'The wife's crook today. She's probably got the wog — there's a lot of it goin' around.'

WOOD

'He's got the wood on me' — he has some kind of advantage over me, which forces me to do whatever he wants me to do.

If your wife knows of some misbehaviour of yours, which she is prepared to forgive and forget provided you 'square off' by taking her out to dinner, or by buying her something she wants, she 'has the wood on you'.

WOULDN'T IT?

An exclamation of astonishment or dismay. Pronounced 'wood'n ut'. Originally 'Wouldn't it root you?', or 'Wouldn't it King Farouk you?'

WOWSER

A character who objects to gambling and drinking — and playing sport on Sunday.

Gamblers and drinkers and advocates of Sunday sport admit the right of any man to refrain from these things, but object to 'wowsers' who try to make *them* refrain.

'The way of the reformer is hard,' it has been said. Profane Aussies reckon it should be made impossible.

The most polite vocal injunction to a crusading wowser is. 'Aw, get off me back, will ya?'

V＊W＊V＊W＊V＊W＊V

YABBER

Small-talk. Yacketty-yak.

'Where're the women?'

'Inside yabberin' their heads off; that's why I come out.' —

'There was an announcement then; what'd he say?'

'Aw, how can a man hear what he says, with all this yabberin' goin' on?'

YAKKER

Work. A tough job is 'hard yakker'.

YIKE

A brawl. A 'blue'.

'Heard there was a big yike up at the pub last night; were you in it?'

'No. I was home, havin' a yike of me own, with the missus.'

90

ZAC

The small coin known otherwise as a sixpence.

'Useless bastards', 'bludgers', 'booze artists', 'bloody dills', 'stupid drongoes', 'earbashers', 'mug galahs', 'lairs', 'lousy bosses', 'lurk merchants', 'skites', 'winge-ers' and 'wowsers' are 'not worth a zac'.

And if you go far inland, you'll find an awful lot of barren country that's also 'not worth a zac'.

We get some migrants, too, who are not worth a zac. So if you're planning to stay in Australia, and you're not worth a zac, you won't make many friends.

But if you're a 'decent bloke', and a 'good sport', and you're 'not afraid of hard yakker', then come in. You'll be 'more than bloody welcome, mate'.

X∗Y∗Z∗X∗Y∗Z

Postscript

THERE is a misconception, particularly amongst the English, that Australians address each other as 'cobber', or 'digger'. And in case anyone should feel annoyed at the omission of these words from the text, reference should be made to them.

The word 'cobber', once extensively used, has been supplanted by the word 'mate'. You can wander around and through this big continent, as the author did recently, without hearing 'cobber' used by anybody, anywhere. No doubt it survives in the speech of isolated individuals, but generally it is as 'dead as a door-nail'.

The same can be said of 'digger', or 'dig', which did not long survive the '14-'18 war. Originally applied to the gold-miners of the nineteenth century, it became a general term of address for the troops of the 1st A.I.F. But it is now 'out' — as are 'bosker', and 'bonzer', of the same vintage.

'He's a bonzer cobber' would now be 'He's a beaut mate'. And 'G'day, dig, how's she goin'?' has become 'Howyagoin' mate, orright?'

Conversation Pieces

AUSSIE English, like any living language, is constantly changing. New meanings are being found for old words; new idiomatic phrases are being developed; new words are invented, or adopted — and many of them go. But some remain and become part of the language.

The words listed, and the quoted examples of their usage, are only those which have been in existence for many years, and which are likely to be in existence for many more. A word can be like 'a poor player, who struts and frets his hour upon the stage, and then is heard no more'. And only posterity can judge whether words will disappear, or become parts of speech.

The same can be said of idiomatic phrases. But the 'speech of the common man', as it is today, and as it will certainly be for some years after this book is published, should be recorded. And the following examples, taken from the author's notes and tapes, are completely authentic:

SYDNEY

Little fellow, very drunk, barging into crowded bar, demands:

'Give us a double sweet sherry.' He knocks over a big fellow's beer.

Big fellow: 'Now look what you done. Man oughta do ya.'

Little fellow (shaping up): 'Fight ya. Fight any bastard who wants to do me.'

Big fellow: 'Aw, you couldn't fight in a fit.'

Little fellow: 'Had a fit once. Had a fight too. Got done over.'

Big fellow (interested): 'I've never had a fit. What's it like?'

They discuss fits, and *both* drink double sweet sherries.

SYDNEY

'Yeah, I agree with you — most barmen are all right. But you take yesterdy. Rainin' like a bastard, an' I get a puncture. Time I get the wheel changed, I'm wet to the arse. Only one thing to do — hit yaself with a couple, right? So I go into this pub. An' there's this smart-aleck galah behind the bar — stupid grin on his dial. "Think it'll rain?" he sez. I sez "Give us a beer" — ignorin' him, like, see? He sez "What you want's a rum." I sez "I know what I bloody want; give us a beer." "New or old?" he sez. "Fifty," I sez. "Yer a bit wet," he sez. I sez "So're you."

94

"Orright," he sez. "Keep ya shirt on." Keep it on? Fair dinkum, it was stickin' to me worse than me mother-in-law.'

MELBOURNE
'Where ya been?'

'Buggerizin' round up in Sydney. Bloody madhouse, that place. They're gettin' more like the Yanks every day. Runnin' round like blue-arsed flies. Dunno whether they're Arthur or Martha half the time. Bloke sez to me — you wouldn't read about this — "Come from Melbourne," he sez. "Yeah," I sez. "What about it?" "Nothin'," he sez. "Prob'ly not your fault. How's yer bridge?" I sez "How's yer opera house?" That shut him up. Got tickets on 'emselves, that mob. You gotta squash 'em.'

MELBOURNE
'Goin' out Saturday?'

'Bloody oath. I'll be there.'
'Got some good information?'
'No. Gave that bloke away. Gettin' me own info now.'
'What, with a pin?'
'No, not with a bloody pin. I'm workin' a system.'
'Gees, that's a good way to go broke.'
'Not this system, mate. This one can't miss.'
'Famous last words. Where do we send the flowers?'

BUSH
'Swaggie' — 'sundowner' — 'hobo' — on the road.

Self: 'G'day, mate. How's she goin'?'

Swaggie: 'Not bad. Don't s'pose ya wouldn't have a smoke on ya, would ya?'

'Sure.'

'Thanks. I've jist run out.'

'Where're you makin' for?'

'Aw, no place in particular.'

'Well, what happens after you get there?'

'I've been, that's what happens.'

BUSH PUB

Little old fellow, wearing suit and tie.

Self: 'See you're all laired up, mate. Goin' somewhere?'

Old fellow: 'No, just been. Picnic races.'

Bloke in shorts: 'Done up like a pox-doctor's clerk, ain't he?'

Old fellow: 'Them doctors. I had three coronaries, ya know. Docs say no more drivin' by yourself, no more races, no more beer.'

'So you drive yourself to the races, and then drink beer.'

'Yeah. Mind you, docs are orright when you get 'em on their own. It's when they start talkin' about ya health is when they drive ya mad.'

BUSH PUB

Big fellow, glass of beer in his hand, says, 'I don't hold with pubs. They're the ruination o' good men. See that young bloke over there? Got a lovely family, an' what does he do? Drink, feed, fight, an' fornicate, that's what.'

'How does he live?'

'Got a small mob o' sheep on the long paddick. Now if it wasn't for pubs he'd be doin' his drinkin' at home, an' lookin' after his family, wouldn't he?'

(Note: The 'long paddock' is the open road.)

96

BUSH PUB

Tall, lean, sunburnt character, wearing a yard-wide hat, is drinking beer with a chubby friend.

'Well,' says chubby, 'gotta leave ya.'

'Eh?' says tall and lean, horrified. 'Gotta leave?'

'Only temporary, like.'

'Gees, you had me worried. Thought ya was goin' home. Have another one?'

'Yeah, when I get back.' He goes.

Tall and lean says, 'Man'll get ulcers worryin' about that feller. He does things sudden. Like goin' home. Like last weekend he lines up on a sheila from the big smoke. Could've ended up married any tick o' the clock.'

'Why do you worry about him?'

'He's me mate.'

It's a flat statement, explaining everything.

COUNTRY TOWN

Middle-aged, dried-up little bloke asks, 'You ever been to Canberra?'

'Yes. Been there often.'

'I'm there last week, for the first time. Full of inter-coorsin' politicians. I'd sooner have in me nostrils the smell o' dead men than the smell of intercoorsin' hope-they-die bloody politicians. They ruin a place. Had to drive fifteen intercoorsin' miles to get a carton o' milk on Sundy. Man shoulda milked some o' them cows in Parliament.'

OUTBACK TOWN

Long, lean, Beatle-headed stockman 'in from up the line'. Not sober.

Self: 'What're you doing in town?'

'Havin' a week's booze-up before takin' another job. Start next Mondy. Started drinkin' soon as I got on the train. Bottle o' rum in me. I'm a bit full now, an' I'm stayin' that way till Sundy. Won't be like a bloke I worked with once, but. Five hundred convictions for bein' drunk last time I seen 'im.'

'How many have you had?'

'Aw, I'm not in his class. I've only had fifteen.'

'Reckon you might improve your average this week?'

'Yeah — might. Feel like havin' a go at a cop. Seen any around?'

OUTBACK TOWN

Self, to manageress of pub: 'Those are nice plastic covers you have on the beds.'

'Aw, ya gotta have 'em here, love. They come in from the stations, ya know, all dusty an' dirty an' dry as the creek. All they want is beer, an' plenty of it. An' *then* all they want's a bit of a lie down before they line up for tucker.'

'With their boots on, eh?'

'Boots on? They don't even take their bloody spurs orf.'

NORTHERN TERRITORY

'Died o' the grog? No, you got it wrong. It wasn't the rum killed 'im. After he buggered that pub up, he got another one, an' buggered that up. Then he come over here an' got himself a good job. An' it wasn't long before he buggered *that* up. Then he meets this sort from down south, all arse an' teeth an' a few quid, an' she buggered *him* up. That's what killed 'im.'

NORTH QUEENSLAND

Middle-aged, motherly lady, discussing local 'characters':
'Did I tell you about me father-in-law an' the horse?'
   'No.'
   'Well, he's cutting the coffee trees with the clippers, see, an' the horse keeps butting in. So he does his block an' throws the clippers at it, an' they stuck fair in his belly. An' woosh — all the air comes out of him. "Get a needle an' twine," he says, "an' sew the bastard up." I says, "He's gunna die — all the air's out of him." An' it was, too. He died. So me father-in-law digs a hole an' rolls him in. But he didn't dig it deep enough, an' there's the horse's four legs sticking up. He gets a saw, an' saws them off. "You're a cruel old man," I says. He says, "What's up with you? How can you be cruel to a dead horse?" '

ISLAND OFF QUEENSLAND COAST

Team with drilling rig, boring for water. Big bony bloke says, 'We're in slate now. You reckon there's water under slate?'
   'Shouldn't think so.'
   'Neither shouldn't bloody I. But we'll keep goin' till we bottom the bastard. Then we're headin' for the Territory. Can't walk around this place now without treadin' on some gink carryin' a camera an' askin' silly bloody questions. Like an old sheila yesterdy. "What're ya doin'?" she says. "Borin' for oil," I says. "Oh," she says, "how do you know it's down there?" I says, "We went down an' had a look, love." Serve 'er bloody right, don't ya reckon?'

Are you 'on to it' now? Are you 'clued up'? If you're

not, then further samples won't do you any good; and if you are, you don't need them. You'll have more fun collecting your own.

Just a final bit of advance information: You'll notice the accent wherever you go, but if you move in business and professional circles you won't hear much of the type of language quoted. On the other hand, out amongst 'the mob', the great majority, the ordinary people, you'll hear plenty. You'll hear it all the time.

And beneath the tongues that speak what may seem to you to be a foreign language, you'll find 'hearts in the right place'. You'll find friendliness and hospitality and a readiness to 'put up with' you that could be surprising.

Good luck to you. And if you don't stay with us permanently — come again. We'll always find a bed for you somewhere, even if one of us has to 'doss on the floor'.

'So long. Be seein' ya.'

&*&*&*&*&*&

Index

102